SCORE SHEET

Name of Game ______________________

Word	Individual/Team 1		Individual/Team 2	
	Reading	Translating	Reading	Translating
1				
2				
3				
4				
5				
6				
7				
8				
9				
10				
11				
12				

BOOK 3

Lesson 6

נְקַדֵּשׁ

שִׁמְךָ

כְּבוֹדוֹ

יִמְלֹךְ

לְדוֹר וָדוֹר

נַגִּיד

גָּדְלֶךָ

וְשִׁבְחֲךָ

Lesson 7

רָב

עַמְּךָ

וְטוֹב

בְּעֵינֶיךָ

לְבָרֵךְ

בִּשְׁלוֹמֶךָ

שִׂים

טוֹבָה

חֵן

אָבִינוּ

כֻּלָּנוּ כְּאֶחָד

נָתַתָּ

תּוֹרַת חַיִּים

וְאַהֲבַת חֶסֶד

Lesson 8

בָּחַר

בִּנְבִיאִים

טוֹבִים

הַנֶּאֱמָרִים

בֶּאֱמֶת

הַבּוֹחֵר

עַבְדּוֹ

עַמּוֹ

וָצֶדֶק

צַדִּיק

הַדּוֹרוֹת

הַנֶּאֱמָן

הָאוֹמֵר

וְעוֹשֶׂה

הַמְדַבֵּר

Lesson 9

הַלְלוּ

עַבְדֵי יְיָ

בְּצֵאת יִשְׂרָאֵל

הוֹדוּ

צַדִּיקִים

בְּעֵינֵינוּ

הַיּוֹם

וְנִשְׂמְחָה

BOOK 3

Lesson 1

לְכָה

דוֹדִי

כַּלָּה

פְּנֵי

נְקַבְּלָה

שָׁמוֹר

זָכוֹר

בֹּאִי

Lesson 2

וְשָׁמְרוּ

בְנֵי

יִשְׂרָאֵל

לַעֲשׂוֹת

לְדֹרֹתָם

בְּרִית

עוֹלָם

הַשָּׁמַיִם

הָאָרֶץ

שָׁבַת

Lesson 3

שָׁלוֹם

עֲלֵיכֶם

מַלְאֲכֵי

עֶלְיוֹן

מֶלֶךְ מַלְכֵי הַמְּלָכִים

הַקָּדוֹשׁ בָּרוּךְ הוּא

בּוֹאֲכֶם

בָּרְכוּנִי

צֵאתְכֶם

Lesson 4

מַה

טֹּבוּ

אֹהָלֶיךָ

וַאֲנִי

חַסְדְּךָ

בֵּיתֶךָ

אָהַבְתִּי

עֹשִׂי

תְפִלָּתִי

יִשְׁעֶךָ

Lesson 5

אַתָּה

גִּבּוֹר

לְעוֹלָם

מְחַיֵּה

הַכֹּל

לְהוֹשִׁיעַ

חַיִּים

בְּרַחֲמִים

מִי כָמוֹךָ

BOOK 2

Lesson 6

וְזֹאת

שָׂם

מֹשֶׁה

לִפְנֵי

בְּנֵי

עֵץ

חַיִּים

מְאֻשָּׁר

דְּרָכֶיהָ

דַרְכֵי

נֹעַם

עַל

שְׁלשָׁה

דְבָרִים

הָעוֹלָם

עוֹמֵד

הַתּוֹרָה

הָעֲבוֹדָה

גְּמִילוּת חֲסָדִים

Lesson 7

עָלֵינוּ

לְשַׁבֵּחַ

לַאֲדוֹן

הַכֹּל

וַאֲנַחְנוּ

וּמוֹדִים

מֶלֶךְ מַלְכֵי הַמְּלָכִים

הָאָרֶץ

בַּיּוֹם הַהוּא

יִהְיֶה

Lesson 8

קַדִּישׁ

יִתְגַּדַּל

וְיִתְקַדַּשׁ

שְׁמֵהּ

בְּעָלְמָא

וְיַמְלִיךְ

מַלְכוּתֵהּ

וּבְחַיֵּי

לְעָלַם

וְיִשְׁתַּבַּח

בְּרִיךְ

בִּרְכָתָא

שְׁלָמָא

Lesson 9

אֵין כ

מִי כ

נוֹדֶה ל

אַתָּה הוּא

אֲדוֹנֵינוּ

מַלְכֵּנוּ

מוֹשִׁיעֵנוּ

BOOK 2

Lesson 1

אָבוֹת

אֵל

אֱלֹהֵי

אֱלֹהֵינוּ

אֲבוֹתֵינוּ

אַבְרָהָם

יִצְחָק

יַעֲקֹב

חֲסָדִים טוֹבִים

חַסְדֵי אָבוֹת

Lesson 2

הָאֵל

הַגָּדוֹל

הַגִּבּוֹר

וְהַנּוֹרָא

עֶלְיוֹן

מֶלֶךְ

עוֹזֵר

וּמוֹשִׁיעַ

וּמָגֵן

Lesson 3

עֹשֶׂה

שָׁלוֹם

יַעֲשֶׂה

עָלֵינוּ

וְעַל

כָּל

יִשְׂרָאֵל

וְאִמְרוּ

אָמֵן

Lesson 4

מִצִּיּוֹן

תּוֹרָה

וּדְבַר

מִירוּשָׁלָיִם

שֶׁנָּתַן

לְעַמּוֹ

בִּקְדֻשָּׁתוֹ

Lesson 5

בָּחַר

בָּנוּ

מִכָּל

הָעַמִּים

וְנָתַן

לָנוּ

תּוֹרָתוֹ

נוֹתֵן

תּוֹרַת

אֱמֶת

וְחַיֵּי

עוֹלָם

BOOK 1

זֵכֶר

לִיצִיאַת מִצְרָיִם

Lesson 9

בְּאַהֲבָה

וּבְרָצוֹן

בָּנוּ

בָחַרְתָּ

וְאוֹתָנוּ קִדַּשְׁתָּ

מִכָּל הָעַמִּים

BOOK 1

Lesson 1

בָּרְכוּ

אֶת

יְיָ

הַמְבֹרָךְ

בָּרוּךְ

לְעוֹלָם וָעֶד

Lesson 2

שְׁמַע

יִשְׂרָאֵל

אֱלֹהֵינוּ

אֶחָד

Lesson 3

שֵׁם

כְּבוֹד

מַלְכוּתוֹ

Lesson 4

מִי

כָמֹכָה, כָּמֹכָה

בָּאֵלִם

נֶאְדָּר

בַּקֹּדֶשׁ

Lesson 5

אַתָּה

מֶלֶךְ

הָעוֹלָם

Lesson 6

אֲשֶׁר

קִדְּשָׁנוּ

בְּמִצְוֹתָיו

וְצִוָּנוּ

Lesson 7

לְהַדְלִיק

נֵר

שֶׁל

שַׁבָּת

בּוֹרֵא

פְּרִי

הַגָּפֶן

הַמּוֹצִיא

לֶחֶם

מִן

הָאָרֶץ

Lesson 8

קִדּוּשׁ

זִכָּרוֹן

לְמַעֲשֵׂה בְרֵאשִׁית

Vocabulary List for *Hebrew Through Prayer* Books 1, 2, and 3

Select the words you want to review with your students. Photocopy and paste them onto the gamesheet of your choice, or write the words in the appropriate spaces. (Your students can do this, too!)

SpeedWay

How to Play

Individuals or teams choose driver 1 or 2. Taking turns, read and translate that driver's six Hebrew words correctly to win the race.

Now try completing the race in reverse.

Go Gefilte Fish

How to Play

Individuals or teams choose fisherman 1 or 2.
Taking turns, read that fisherman's six Hebrew words to catch a fish.
Then switch and read the other fisherman's words.
Now play the game again, this time by translating the words to catch a fish.

7	1
8	2
9	3
10	4
11	5
12	6

PAR-PAR GOLF

How to Play

Individuals or teams each start the game with 18 points. Take turns reading and translating each Hebrew word. Deduct one point for each word read correctly. Deduct another point for each word translated correctly. The individual or team with the lowest score wins.

OLYMPIC RELAYS

How to Play
Individuals or teams choose
runner 1 or 2.
Taking turns, read that runner's
six Hebrew words to run the race
and cross the finish line.
Then switch and read
the other runner's words.
Now play the game
by translating the words.

1

2

3

4

5

6

7

8

9

10

11

12

Treasure Island

How to Play

Read and translate the Hebrew words along the path to find the pirates' treasure.

Surf's Up

How to Play

Individuals or teams choose surfer 1 or 2.
Taking turns, read and translate that surfer's six Hebrew words to ride a wave to shore.
Then switch and read the other surfer's words.

Crown Jewels

How to Play

Partner 1 reads a word.
Partner 2 translates the same word.
Partners then switch the reading and translating.
When a word has been read and translated correctly, color its jewel.

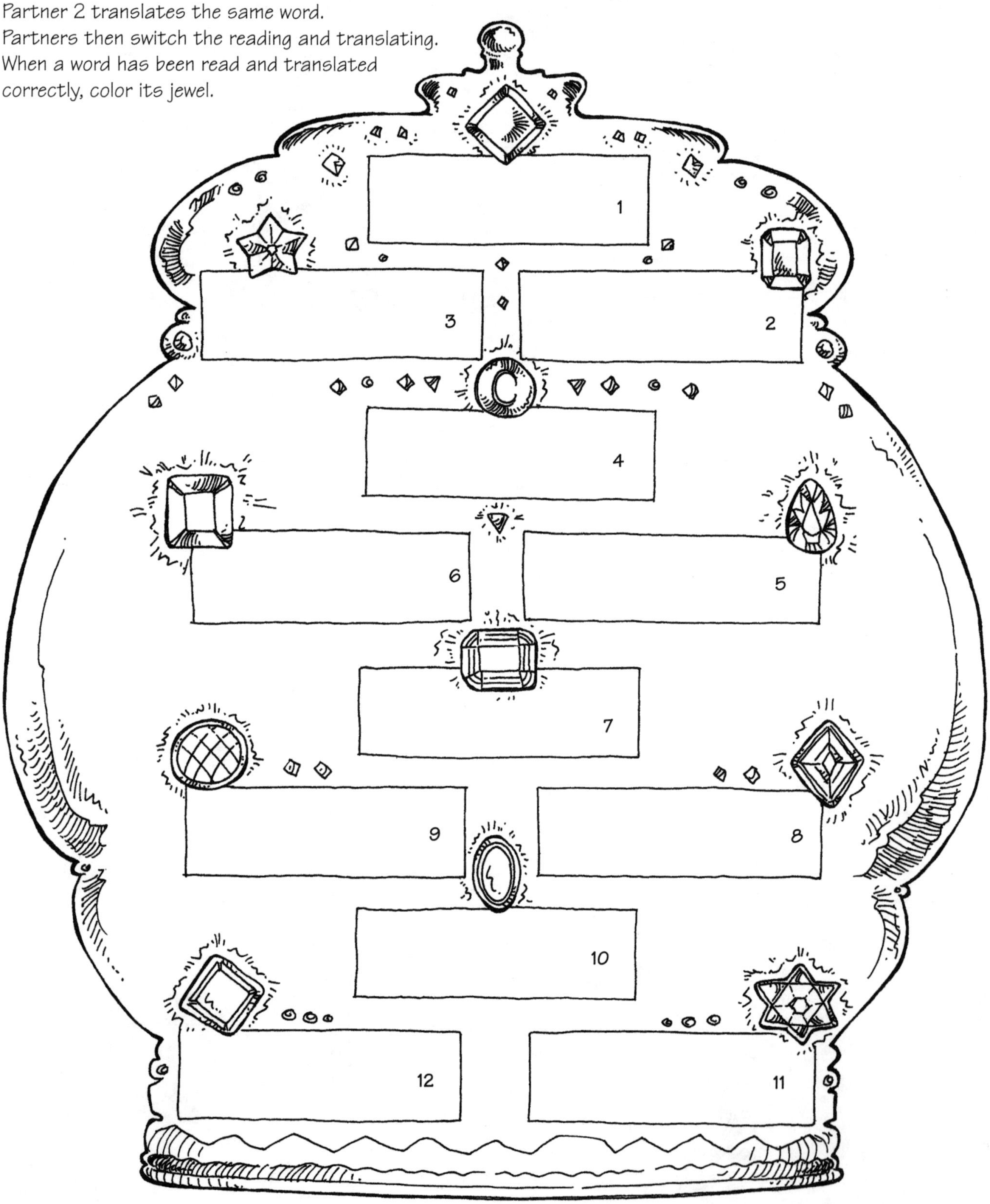

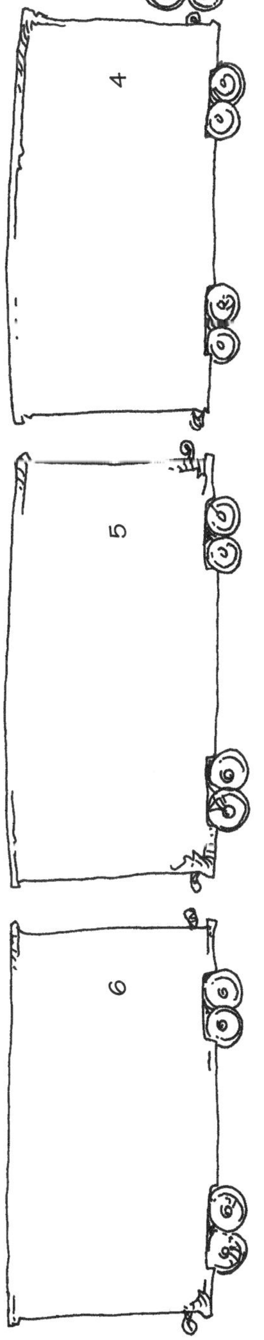

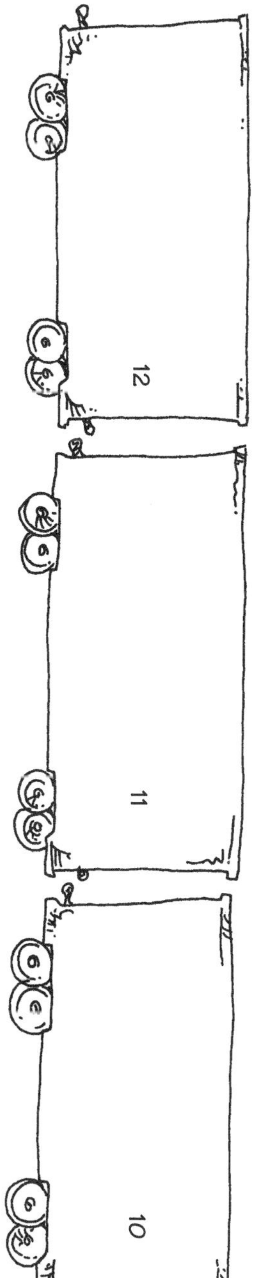

Train Game

How to Play

Individual or Team 1 reads and translates the first six Hebrew words and connects a train car for each correct word.
Individual or Team 2 reads and translates the last six Hebrew words and connects a train car for each correct word.
Then erase the connecting lines, switch, and read and translate the other team's words.
The individual or team to make the most connections wins.

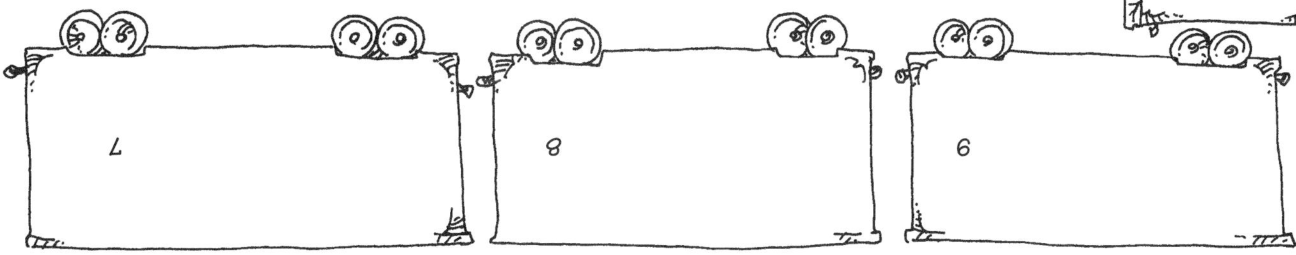

JAFFA PICKERS

How to Play

Individuals or teams take turns "picking oranges" by reading and translating the Hebrew words.
Score one point for each word read correctly.
Score two more points for each word translated correctly.
The individual or team with the most points wins.

Obstacle Course

How to Play

Individuals or teams try to arrive home safely by reading and translating the words along the obstacle course.

Blast Off

How to Play

Individuals or teams take turns "counting down to blast-off" by reading and translating words 1–12 on the rocket. Score one point for each word read correctly. Score two points for each word translated correctly. Then play again by reading the words twelve through one to lift-off.

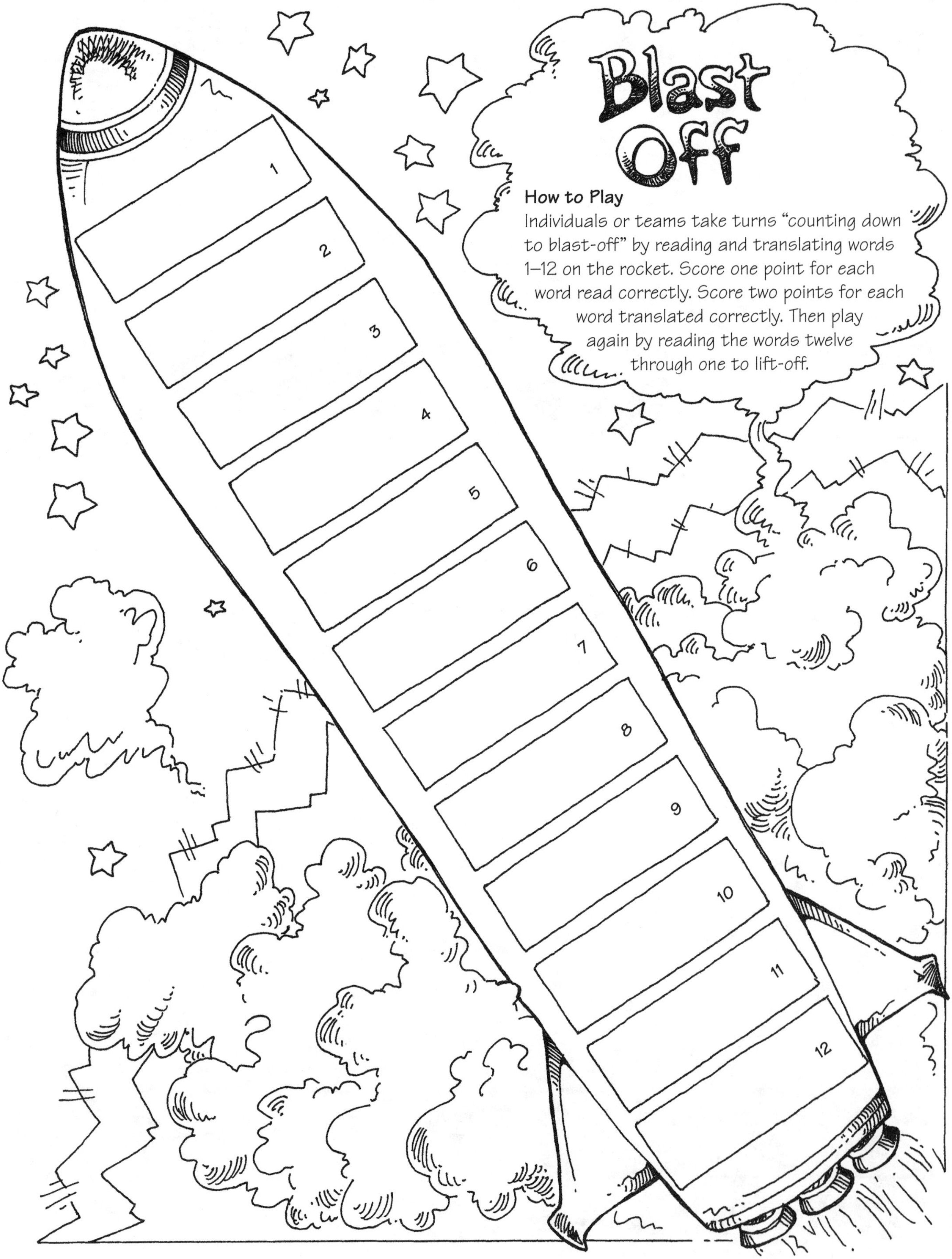

Score One Soccer

7

8

9

10

11

12

How to Play

Individuals or teams choose soccer player 1 or 2. Taking turns, read and translate that soccer player's six Hebrew words to cross the field and score a goal. Then switch and read and translate the other player's six words.

1

2

3

4

5

6

POP THE BALLOON!

How to Play

Individuals or teams take turns "popping the balloons" by reading and translating the Hebrew words. Score one point for each word read correctly. Score two more points for each word translated correctly. The individual or team with the most points wins.

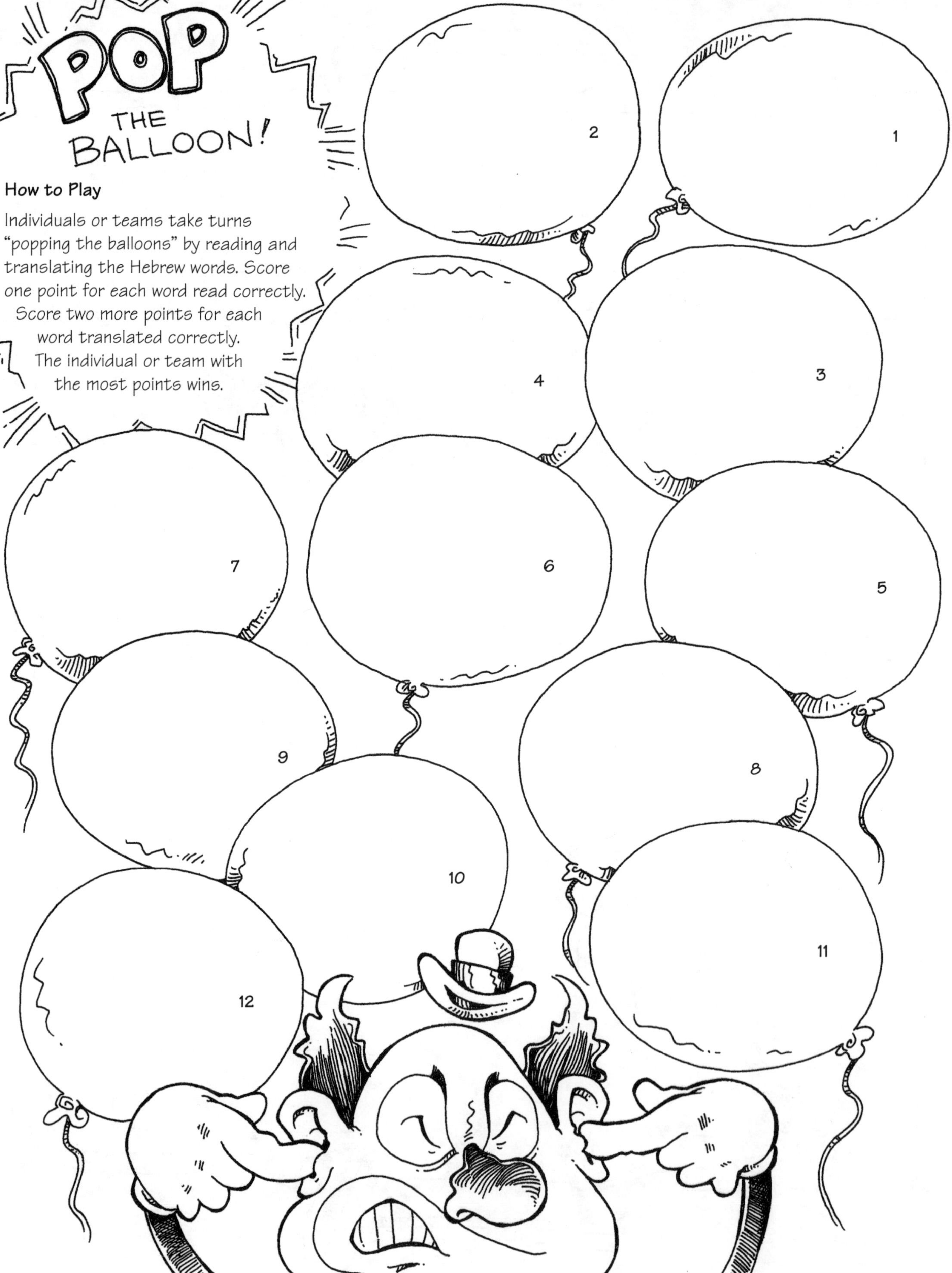

Word Toss

How to Play

Individuals or teams toss a paper clip onto the gamesheet. Read the Hebrew word closest to the paper clip to score one point. Translate the word to score two more points. Then cross out the word. Play until all the words have been read. The individual or team with the most points wins.

Leap Frog

How to Play

Individuals or teams take turns reading and translating each Hebrew word.
Score one point for each word read correctly.
Score two more points for each word translated correctly.
The individual or team with the most points wins.

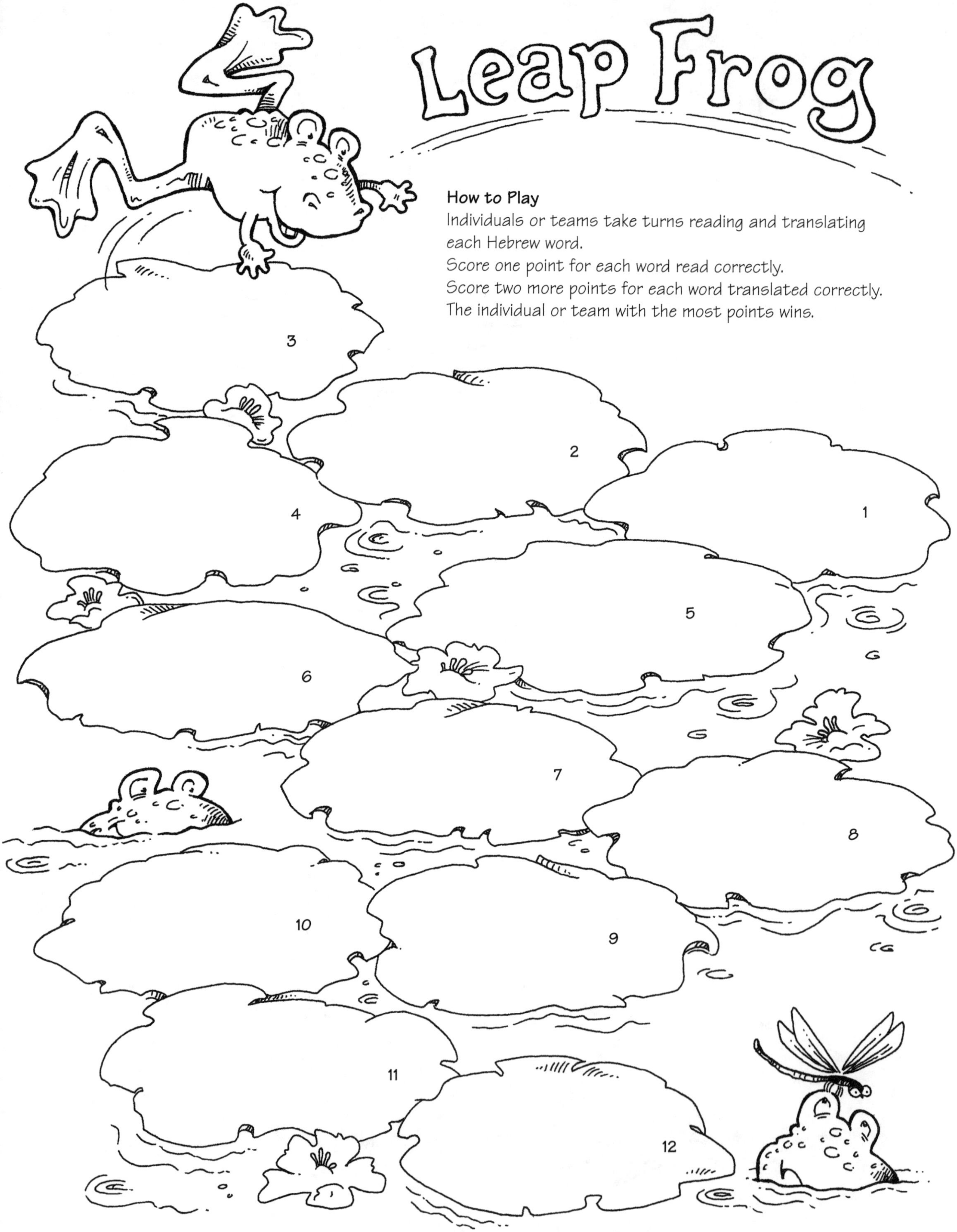

Section II

Create-Your-Own Games

Blank gamesheets allow you to select the Hebrew words you want to review. A vocabulary list for *Hebrew Through Prayer Books 1, 2,* and *3* appears at the end of this section. To create a game, photocopy the blank gamesheet of your choice. Then select the words you want to review. Photocopy and paste them onto the sheet or write them in the appropriate spaces. Finally, duplicate a copy of your customized game for each student and follow the instructions for play.

12 הַיּוֹם

11 הוֹדוּ

10 בְּצֵאת יִשְׂרָאֵל

9 עַבְדֵי יְיָ

8 הַלְלוּ

7 הַדּוֹרוֹת

SPEEDWAY

When to Play

Book 3, Lesson 9

How to Play

Individuals or teams choose driver 1 or 2. Taking turns, read and translate that driver's six Hebrew words correctly to win the race.

Now try completing the race in reverse.

1 בָּחַר

2 בִּנְבִיאִים

3 טוֹבִים

4 בֶּאֱמֶת

5 עַמּוֹ

6 צַדִּיק

Go Gefilte Fish

When to Play
Book 3, Lesson 7

How to Play
Individuals or teams choose fisherman 1 or 2. Taking turns, read that fisherman's six Hebrew words to catch a fish. Then switch and read the other fisherman's words. Now play the game again, this time by translating the words to catch a fish.

	Fisherman 2		Fisherman 1
7	שִׂים	1	רָב
8	טוֹבָה	2	עַמְּךָ
9	חֵן	3	וְטוֹב
10	אָבִינוּ	4	בְּעֵינֶיךָ
11	תּוֹרַת חַיִּים	5	לְבָרֵךְ
12	וְאַהֲבַת חֶסֶד	6	בִּשְׁלוֹמֶךָ

PAR·PAR GOLF

When to Play
Book 3, Lesson 6

How to Play
Individuals or teams each start the game with 18 points. Take turns reading and translating each Hebrew word. Deduct one point for each word read correctly. Deduct another point for each word translated correctly. The individual or team with the lowest score wins.

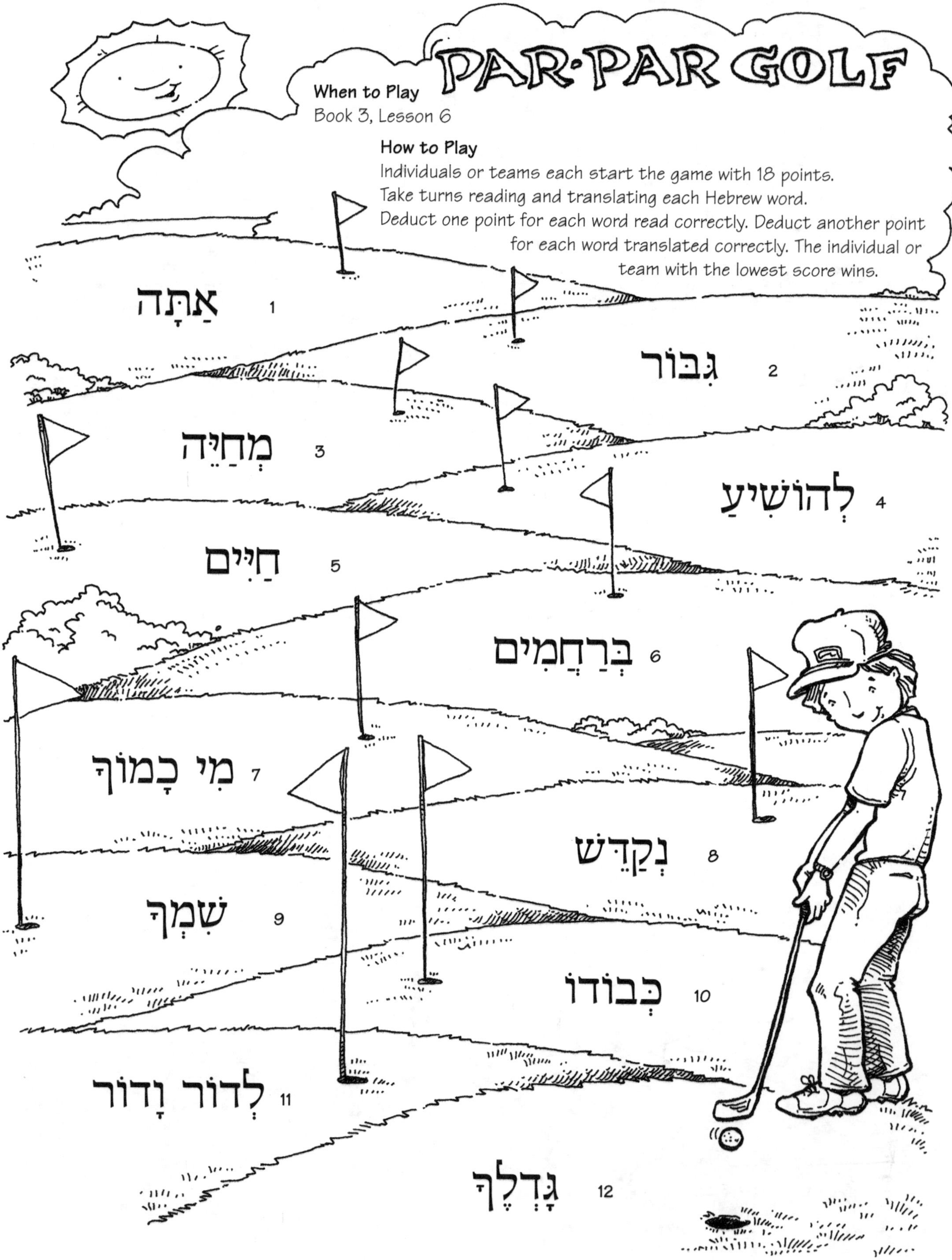

1 אַתָּה

2 גִּבּוֹר

3 מְחַיֵּה

4 לְהוֹשִׁיעַ

5 חַיִּים

6 בְּרַחֲמִים

7 מִי כָמוֹךָ

8 נְקַדֵּשׁ

9 שִׁמְךָ

10 כְּבוֹדוֹ

11 לְדוֹר וָדוֹר

12 גָּדְלֶךָ

OLYMPIC RELAYS

When to Play

Book 3, Lesson 4

How to Play

Individuals or teams choose runner 1 or 2.
Taking turns, read that runner's six Hebrew words to run the race and cross the finish line.
Then switch and read the other runner's words.
Now play the game by translating the words.

1 עֲלֵיכֶם	7 צֵאתְכֶם
2 מַלְאֲכֵי	8 טֹבוּ
3 עֶלְיוֹן	9 וַאֲנִי
4 הַקָּדוֹשׁ בָּרוּךְ הוּא	10 בֵּיתֶךָ
5 בּוֹאֲכֶם	11 אָהַבְתִּי
6 בָּרְכוּנִי	12 תְּפִלָּתִי

Treasure Island

When to Play

Book 3, Lesson 2

How to Play

Read and translate the Hebrew words along the path to find the pirates' treasure.

Surf's Up

When to Play

Book 2, Lesson 9

How to Play

Individuals or teams choose surfer 1 or 2. Taking turns, read and translate that surfer's six Hebrew words to ride a wave to shore.

Then switch and read the other surfer's words.

1 עֹשֶׂה שָׁלוֹם

2 עָלֵינוּ

3 כָּל

4 יִשְׂרָאֵל

5 אֵין כּ

6 מִי כ

7 נוֹדֶה ל

8 אַתָּה

9 אֱלֹהֵינוּ

10 אֲדוֹנֵינוּ

11 מַלְכֵּנוּ

12 מוֹשִׁיעֵנוּ

Crown Jewels

When to Play
Book 2, Lesson 8

How to Play
Partner 1 reads a word.
Partner 2 translates the same word.
Partners then switch the reading and translating.
When a word has been read and translated correctly, color its jewel.

1 שָׁם

2 מֹשֶׁה

3 לִפְנֵי

4 בְּנֵי

5 עֵץ

6 חַיִּים

7 שְׁלֹשָׁה

8 דְּבָרִים

9 הָעוֹלָם

10 עוֹמֵד

11 הָעֲבוֹדָה

12 גְּמִילוּת חֲסָדִים

Train Game

When to Play

Book 2, Lesson 6

How to Play

Individual or Team 1 reads and translates the first six Hebrew words and connects a train car for each correct word.
Individual or Team 2 reads and translates the last six Hebrew words and connects a train car for each correct word.
Then erase the connecting lines, switch, and read and translate the other team's words.
The individual or team to make the most connections wins.

Jaffa Pickers

When to Play
Book 2, Lesson 5

How to Play
Individuals or teams take turns "picking oranges" by reading and translating the Hebrew words.
Score one point for each word read correctly.
Score two more points for each word translated correctly.
The individual or team with the most points wins.

1 בָּרְכוּ
2 בָּחַר
3 מִכָּל
4 הָעַמִּים
5 וְנָתַן
6 לָנוּ
7 תּוֹרָתוֹ
8 נוֹתֵן
9 אֱמֶת
10 וְחַיֵּי
11 עוֹלָם
12 עֲלִיָּה

Obstacle Course

When to Play

Book 2, Lesson 4

How to Play

Individuals or teams try to arrive home safely by reading and translating the words along the obstacle course.

Blast Off

When to Play
Book 2, Lesson 2

How to Play
Individuals or teams take turns “counting down to blast-off” by reading and translating words 1–12 on the rocket. Score one point for each word read correctly. Score two points for each word translated correctly. Then play again by reading the words twelve through one to lift-off.

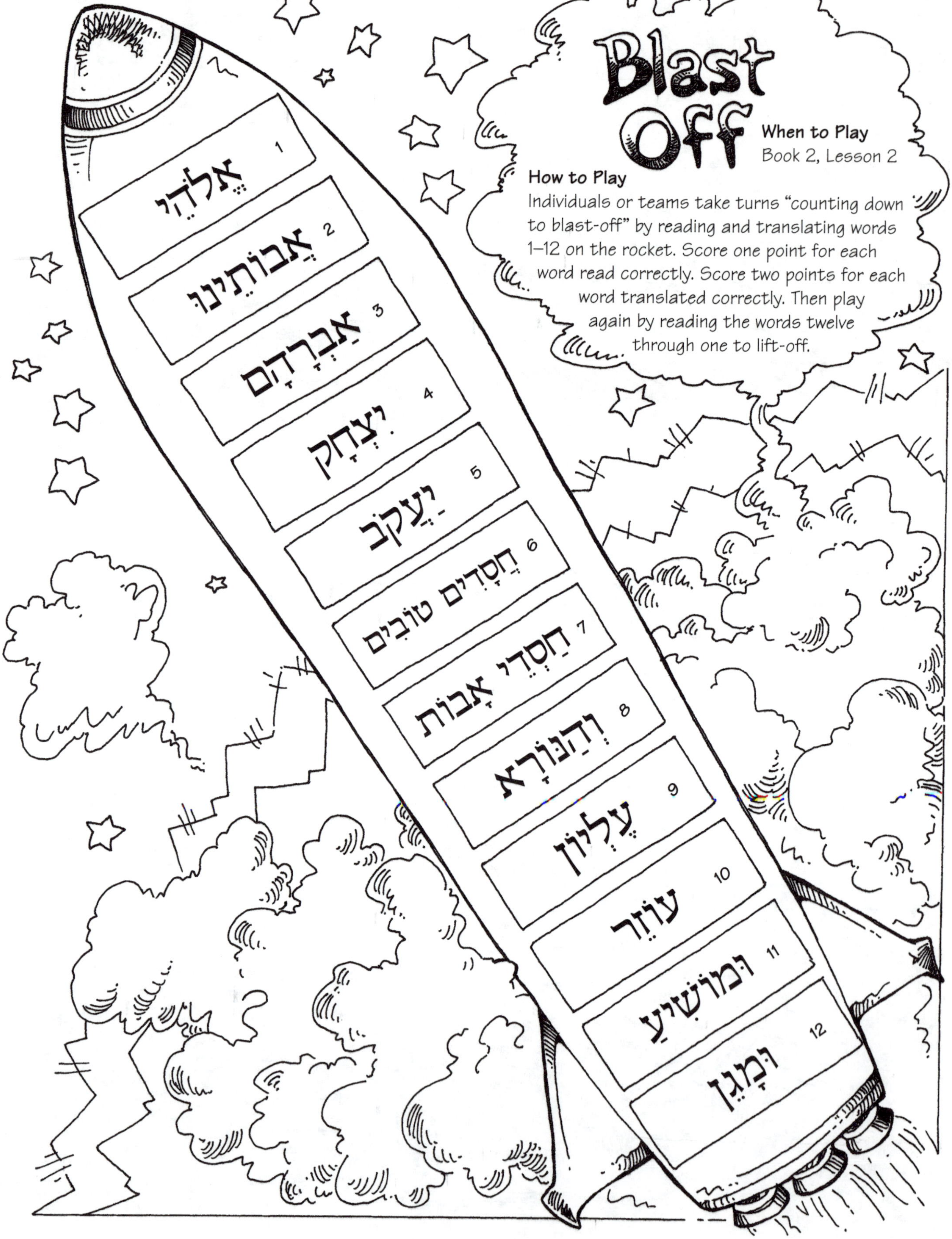

Score One Soccer

When to Play

Book 1, Lesson 9

How to Play

Individuals or teams choose soccer player 1 or 2. Taking turns, read and translate that soccer player's six Hebrew words to cross the field and score a goal. Then switch and read and translate the other player's six words.

1 קְדוֹשׁ

2 זִכָּרוֹן

3 לְמַעֲשֵׂה בְרֵאשִׁית

4 זֵכֶר

5 לִיצִיאַת מִצְרָיִם

6 בְּאַהֲבָה

7 וּבְרָצוֹן

8 בָנוּ

9 בָחַרְתָּ

10 וְאוֹתָנוּ קִדַּשְׁתָּ

11 מִכָּל הָעַמִּים

12 יִשְׂרָאֵל

POP THE BALLOON!

When to Play Book 1, Lesson 7

How to Play Individuals or teams take turns "popping the balloons" by reading and translating the Hebrew words. Score one point for each word read correctly.

Score two more points for each word translated correctly.

The individual or team with the most points wins.

1 בְּרָכָה

2 לְהַדְלִיק

3 נֵר

4 שֶׁל

5 שַׁבָּת

6 בּוֹרֵא

7 פְּרִי

8 הַגָּפֶן

9 הַמּוֹצִיא

10 לֶחֶם

11 מִן

12 הָאָרֶץ

Word Toss

When to Play Book 1, Lesson 6

How to Play Individuals or teams toss a paper clip onto the gamesheet. Read the Hebrew word closest to the paper clip to score one point. Translate the word to score two more points. Then cross out the word. Play until all the words have been read. The individual or team with the most points wins.

1 מִי

2 כָּמֹכָה

3 בָּאֵלִם

4 נֶאְדָּר

5 בַּקֹּדֶשׁ

6 אַתָּה

7 מֶלֶךְ

8 הָעוֹלָם

9 אֲשֶׁר

10 קִדְּשָׁנוּ

11 בְּמִצְוֹתָיו

12 וְצִוָּנוּ

Leap Frog

When to Play

Book 1, Lesson 3

How to Play

Individuals or teams take turns reading and translating each Hebrew word.
Score one point for each word read correctly.
Score two more points for each word translated correctly.
The individual or team with the most points wins.

Section I

Classroom-Ready Games

Each gamesheet tells you when to play the game. Gamesheets contain words students have learned in preceding lessons. Duplicate a gamesheet for each student and follow the instructions for play. Instructions allow for flexible play.

To the Teacher:

Hebrew Through Prayer is a three-year program to teach students key prayers in the Shabbat Morning Service, the Friday Evening Service, *Hallel*, and the essential prayers and blessings for home observance. This book of black-line masters contains classroom games to review the vocabulary in *Hebrew Through Prayer Books 1, 2,* and *3*. The book contains 15 classroom-ready games and 15 create-your-own games to personalize. You will find a score sheet on the last page of this book.

How to use the classroom-ready games (Section I):

Each gamesheet tells you when to play the game. For example, play "Pop the Balloon" after completing *Book 1,* Lesson 7. This gamesheet contains words students have learned in preceding lessons. Duplicate a gamesheet for each student and follow the instructions for play. Students can play as individuals, as members of a team, or as a class. All games require students to read and translate key prayer words, but not every game calls for a "winner." The instructions allow for flexible play and student involvement. Students can decide how many times to play a game, whether to read all the words and *then* translate them, and whether an incorrect answer means loss of a point, forfeiting a turn, or no loss at all.

How to create your own games (Section II):

Blank gamesheets allow you to select the Hebrew words you want to review. A vocabulary list for *Hebrew Through Prayer Books 1, 2,* and *3* appears at the end of this section. To create a game, photocopy the blank gamesheet of your choice. Then select the words you want to review. Photocopy and paste them onto the sheet or write them in the appropriate spaces. Finally, duplicate a copy of your customized game for each student and follow the instructions for play.

The games facilitate learning in several ways. They:

- provide practice and review in reading and translating
- give students opportunities for active participation
- reinforce learning in a relaxed setting
- relieve the monotony of necessary drill
- encourage students to work cooperatively

We are eager to hear your reactions to these materials. Please write or call to let us know what worked best for you and your students.

B'hatslaḥah,

Terry Kaye
Hebrew Curriculum Consultant
Behrman House

STUDENT GAMES
HEBREW THROUGH PRAYER
BOOKS 1, 2, and 3

BLACK-LINE MASTERS

by
Shoshana Silberman

Illustrations
Larry Nolte

235 Watchung Avenue, West Orange, New Jersey 07052
ISBN: 0-87441-659-0
MANUFACTURED IN THE UNITED STATES OF AMERICA